SCHIRMER'S LIBRARY
OF MUSICAL CLASSICS

Vol. 749

CARL CZERNY

Op. 453

One Hundred and Ten Easy and Progressive Exercises

For Pianoforte

**Edited and Fingered
By
GIUSEPPE BUONAMICI**

G. SCHIRMER, Inc.

DISTRIBUTED BY

HAL•LEONARD®
CORPORATION
7777 W. BLUEMOUND RD. P.O. BOX 13819 MILWAUKEE, WI 53213

One Hundred and Ten
Easy and Progressive Exercises.*)

Carl Czerny. Op. 453

*) The pupil should also practise the first fourteen exercises transposed into C♯, employing the same fingering even in places where some difficulty is encountered by doing so.

16693X

8

10

Allegro moderato.

17.

16693

Allegro moderato.

20.

Allegro.

25.

Allegretto moderato.

Andantino con moto.

Allegro moderato.

30.

23

16693

28

16693

30

16693

Allegretto.

54.

Allegretto vivo.

55.

p

legato il basso

Allegro.

56.

D. C. sin' al Fine.

58.

59.

Allegretto vivace.

D. C. sin' al Fine.

Allegro alla marcia.

60.

Fine.

Trio.

p dolce

ff

p

dolce

D.C. sin' al Fine.

46

16898

48

54

Allegretto.

73.

56

Allegretto.

75.

16693

Andantino grazioso.

77.

p dolce delicatamente

79.

Allegretto.

80.

Allegretto.

83.

Allegro maestoso.

84.

Andantino grazioso.

92.

93.

Allegro.

94.

p leggermente e veloce

Molto allegro.

100.

84

104.

16693

86

Allegro vivace.

Andantino.

*) Also practise in C♯ without change of fingering.

16693

Allegro vivace.

108.

Allegro vivace.

109.